This book belongs to:_ _ _ _ _ _ _ _ _ _ _ _ _ _ _ _ _ _ _

This book is dedicated to my son, Kai, thank you for all your inspiration and encouragement.

Kai is about to start school.
He's excited, and a little bit nervous.
"What do I need to bring?" he asks.
His dad is taking him to the store to get pencils, paper,
and a new backpack.

The store is full of school supplies.
"Do I need this?" Kai asks holding up an eraser.
"Let's start with a backpack and a lunchbox," his dad says.
Kai is excited to pick out his new stuff.

There are blue backpacks, pink backpacks, green backpacks and more.
"Which one do you like?"
Kai looks up and down the aisle, but just can't decide.
"Maybe this one?" he says, "oooh I also like this one."

They end up leaving with three bags full of stuff.
A backpack, a lunch box, paper, pencils, markers, even a ruler
and some glue sticks
"I'm ready!" Kai shouts.
Kai is more than prepared.

School starts in three days.
And Kai still has a few things to learn.
"Around the loop and pull it through!" his mom says.
They are working on tying Kai's shoes.

Kai also needs to work on zipping up his jacket by himself.
"Once you figure it out, you'll be part of the zipper club!" Kai's
mom exclaims.
Kai really wants to be a part of the zipper club.
He really wants to be ready for school.

Kai works on his laces and zipper every day.
Tying his shoes and zipping up his jacket until he can do it all by himself.
"You're all set now!" Kai's mom says giving him a high five.
"But what if I don't make any friends?" Kai says with a worried look.

Now that Kai has got his supplies, knows how to tie his shoes, and figured out his zipper, he's starting to worry about what school will be like. "What if my teacher is mean?" he wonders, "what if the classroom is scary?" Kai imagines a dark room with tangled vines covering the walls and monsters hiding under desks.

He pictures his teacher having a grumpy, vampire-looking face,
with red eyes.
"Yikes! I better stay home for another year!" Kai says.
"You can't stay home!" his dad says, "don't worry, everyone feels
a little nervous before the first day of school."

But Kai is more than nervous.
The next morning, he didn't get out of bed.
"I'm sick. I can't go!" he whines as his mom comes into his room.
Kai is too scared and too nervous to go anywhere.

"Don't worry, Kai!" his mom says calmly, I promise everything will be okay."
It takes a bit of convincing, but Kai agrees to get dressed.
"Don't forget to brush your teeth too!" his mom says heading back
downstairs to make breakfast.

11

Kai does his best not to think about the day ahead.
And when it's time to go, he ties his shoes, and zips up his jacket.
"Wow! You did it!" his dad is impressed and so is Kai.
He wasn't even thinking about it, he just did it.

"Maybe I am ready" Kai thinks to himself.
When they get to the school, Kai takes a deep breath.
"I can do this!" he mumbles under his breath.
And it only takes a matter of seconds, for all his fears to crumble.

"You must be Kai!" a cheerful woman with rosy cheeks says with a smile.
Kai looks up with a worried face.
"I'm Mrs. Turnatee, welcome to school!" she says.
Instantly, Kai feels better.
"You're my teacher?" he questions, "you're not scary at all, and you definitely don't look like a vampire!"

Mrs. Turnatee chuckles to herself.
"C'mon, this way!" she says, taking Kai inside.
"Bye, mom, bye, dad!" Kai shouts. He's still worried about what his classroom will be like, but he's feeling comfortable enough to head inside with his teacher. CREAAAAAK
Kai cringes and closes his eyes as Mrs. Turnatee opens the door to the school.

"This is where you'll hang your coat" Mrs. Turnatee says, pointing
to a long row of hooks.
Kai slowly opens his eyes, bracing for a dark, shadowy hallway
full of fear.
But to his surprise, it's bright, colorful, and full of cheer.
"This is my school?" Kai says out loud, in shock.

"And this is your classroom" Mrs. Turnatee says opening the door
to the room.
It's even brighter than the hallway. There are colorful pictures
covering the walls and the chairs and desks are rainbow-colored.
"Did I tell you I love rainbows?" Mrs. Turnatee says, "so much
so that some students call me Mrs. Rainbow!"

Kai is thrilled. He's so relieved he forgets all about his fears. The room slowly fills up with other students, and then the bell rings. BRRRRING!
Kai is more than happy with his school, teacher, and classroom.
"What a pleasant surprise" he thinks to himself.
But he's still worried about making friends.

BRRRRRING! The bell rings again.
"Time for recess!" Mrs. Turnatee shouts, leading her class out to the playground.
"Hi, my name is Theresa" a little girl turns to Kai and says, "do you want to play with me?"
Kai smiles and agrees, not realizing that he has just made a friend.

Kai and Theresa play in the sandbox together, giggling and building sandcastles.
It's so much fun, and Kai can't stop smiling.
Before he knows it, the day is over, and it's time to head back home.

"Kai!" his dad shouts, as he arrives to pick him up, "did you have an okay day?"
"Do I have to go home now?" Kai whines, "I want to stay longer!"
Kai's dad smiles in relief.
He is happy to hear about Kai's fun day.

"Bye Kai!" they hear a little girl shout from behind them, "see you tomorrow."
It's Theresa.
"Is she your new friend?" Kai's dad asks.
"she sure is!" Kai says with a grin, "let's go home, dad. I'll tell you all about it!"